Salvation in a Mystery

By John Bond

Salvation in a Mystery
By John Bond

Edited and updated by C. Matthew McMahon and Therese B. McMahon
Transcribed by Sylvie Vazaios

Published by Puritan Publications
A Ministry of A Puritan's Mind
4101 Coral Tree Circle #214
Coconut Creek, FL 33073
www.puritanpublications.com
www.apuritansmind.com

This hardback first edition, 2012
Electronic Edition, 2012
Manufactured in the United States of America

ISBN: 978-1-938721-11-3
eISBN: 978-1-938721-10-6

CONTENTS

PREFACE

Die Mercurii, 27 Martii, 1644

It is this day ordered by the Commons, assembled in parliament (concerning Master Bond and Master Nicolls) do from this house give thanks to Master Bond for the great pains he took in the discourse he preached at Margaret Westminster at the in treaty of this house (it being the day of public humiliation) and they are to desire him to print his sermon. And it is ordered that none presume to print or reprint his sermon without being authorized under the hand writing of the said Master Bond.

H. Elsynge Cler. Parl. D. Com.

I do appoint Francis Eglesfeild to print my sermon.

John Bond

[Original Title Page]

SALVATION

IN A

MYSTERY

Or
A Prospective Glass
For England's Case.

As it was laid forth in a sermon
preached at MARGARET'S in Westminster,
before the honorable house of Commons,
at their monthly fast,
March 27,
1644.

BY JOHN BOND, B.LL.
late lecturer in the city of Exciter, now
Preacher at the *Savoy* in *London*.
A member of the Assembly of Divines.
Published by order of the commons house.

Exodus 3:2, "The Bush burned with fire, and the bush
was not consumed."
Judges 14:14, "Out of the eater came forth meat, and out
of the strong came forth sweetness."

LONDON,
Printed by L. N. for *Francis Eglesfeild*, and are to be sold at
the sign of the Marygold in Paul's church.
1644.

To The Honorable House of Commons Now Assembled In Parliament

Honorable Worthies:

That which by your first command, was in part, presented to your cares from the pulpit, is here at your second command, fully represented to your eyes from the press. It is a piece, I dare say, a rare and useful piece for the plot and subject, which are immediately the Lord's, as it is plain and homely in my style and method. In its dress, I thought it a duty to put off ornaments; for although it was preached on the yearly day of the King's inauguration, yet that season (March 27th) was also the monthly day of the kingdom's humiliation; when you did endeavor to weep, pray, and fast for the royal family; while others (perhaps at Oxford) did drink, blaspheme, and debauch themselves, to show their loyalty to his majesty.

The subject of this sermon is like the two pillars which guided (our type) Israel through the wilderness to Canaan by day, and night. The one was a cloud, which might well signify the Lord hiding himself. The other of fire, importing him to be the Savior of Israel even while he was in that cloud.

There is much talk now days of new light, and that new light as it is held forth by some, is nothing less than old darkness. I may safely promise you in this treatise, at least, the dawning of a light that is now Orthodox and certain. By which I have endeavored to begin the discovery of a hidden gem of precious providence; though all my labors, have scarcely opened the uppermost surface of the ground. I shall leave the accurate searching of the veins to more able observers.

I confess that I made an essay on this very text, in my native climate, before my banishment; but being plundered of those speculative thoughts; and having, since that time in some measure experimented this text; I conceive myself bound in conscience to give you some meat out of my eater. Surely there is a vast difference between hearing of the Lord by the hearing of the ear and when our eyes have seen him (Job 42:5).

May it please you therefore to travel over this unusual discourse once again; are mysteries commonly are not understood at the first perusal? I am sure that no parliament in England had greater need of Viatica than yourselves. You are made a spectacle to angels and men; and believe it, you are set up, for the fall and rising again of many in England. The Lord has cut off all bridges behind you (and blessed be his name that they are cut off) and now, together with you, all the treasures of great Britain and Ireland are embarked. And according to your standing of falling in this great cause, must the present generation and their posterities in the three kingdoms, begin the dates of their perpetual real or woe; for, pure reformation, or open property, ingenious liberty, or Norman slavery must now be made the settled master. No, to allude to Caesar's speech, you do now carry the whole protestant cause, with all its fortunes.

For my own part, there is nothing on earth, that more amazes my intellectuals, then the prodigious lethargy that still rests on the heads and hearts of cursed neuters, and protestants and malignant in the land, even now when both parties abhor indifference, and that the execrable rebels of Ireland are brought over. But I might silence myself in this *quos perdece vult Jupiter, eos dementat.* Surely the Lord has smitten the generality of the land with madness and blindness and astonishment of heart, as he threatened the Jews. Otherwise they could never dream of defending parliaments by malefactors, property by desperadoes, and Protestantism by Irish rebels. May, we not fear lest the Spanish, or Irish, or other foreigners, may invade the whole land of the King, and obtain it, alleging that the nation, is not *compos mentis*?

But my hope shall be, that after the Lord has deeply humbled us for our old and new abominations, and broken us as he did Nebuchadnezzar (Daniel 4:14), when he has shown us down, cut off our branches, shaken off our leaves, and scattered our fruits; when he has driven us from men, and suffered our heirs (verse 25) to grow like eagles feathers (verse 33), and our nails like birds claws; then at the end of the days, men's reason and understanding shall return to them again, and perhaps, our glory also. At least, I am confident, that God will leave in the middle of us an afflicted and poor people, and they shall trust in the name of the Lord.

Meanwhile, it is my petition to you, and for you (worthy patriots) that you may hold out through all those seas of difficulties which are before you; and that you may remember that God is not unrighteous to forget your work and labor of love, which you have showed toward his name (Heb. 6:10). Yes, you may take it for a positive promise (2 Thess. 3:3). The Lord is faithful, who shall establish you, and keep you from evil; and we have confidence in the Lord, touching you, that you both do (verse 4), and will do, the things which he commands you. And the Lord directs your hearts into the love of God, and into the patient waiting for Christ. This is my fixed hope, and shall ever be my fervent prayer.

From my study at the Savoy,
April 20, 1644.

Your humble and willing servant,
John Bond

PART 1: THE TEXT OPENED

Isaiah 45:15, "Verily, thou art a God that hides thyself, O God of Israel the Savior."

A Discourse Given at a Late Fast,
before the Honorable House of Commons

The spring head of this text (as some conceive) arises at the sixth verse of the 44th chapter. Others fetch it as high as chapter 43 verse 14. "Thus says the Lord your redeemer, the Holy One of Israel; for your sakes I have sent to Babylon." And the streams run down as far as the end of chapter 48. The whole section divides itself into two branches.

The first is a prophetical promise of the return of the Jews from their Babylon's captivity. That ends with the chapter of my text.

And, the second is a prophetical threatening of the downfall of Babylon shortly after that deliverance. This extends from the beginning of the next chapter to the end of this prophesy, chapter 48. (*There is no peace, says the Lord, unto the wicked*).

In this prophetical promissory chapter of my text, commonly three parts or heads are observed.

The first sets forth the principal instrument of this strange gaoler delivery. It is Cyrus the Persian, whom the Lord calls by name to this great service; for instead of *Spacus* that is in the median language Canis, (so called because he had been nursed by a female dog) he is surnamed Coresch by the Persians, which among them signifies *a Lord (Herodotus Justinus)*. This strange man is anointed, that is, authorized and fitted to this strange work. The fitting of him lies in these particulars.

First, in giving strength to him. Wisdom and strength are for the war. The Lord promises to hold his hand as the scribe guides the hand of his unready scholar; or rather as Elisha put his hands on the hands of Joash King of Israel, when he shot the arrow of the Lord's deliverance, the arrow of deliverance from Syria, 2 King 13:16-17. So the expression runs of this prophet, verse 1. "Thus says the Lord to Cyrus, whose right hand I have held."

Next, the Lord does as it were provide pioneers for him to further his march, by opening of gates, leveling of ways, and removing all obstacles and impediments, verse 1. "I will lose the sons of Kings, to open before him the two leaved gates, and the gates shall not be shut," verse 3. "I will go before him, and make the crooked places straight," *etc.*

But there is a third thing yet behind, and that is the sins of war, a sufficient treasury for the work. This also shall be supplied, verse 3. "And I will give you the treasures of darkness and hidden riches of secret places." So the Lord will be the victor of auxiliaries, of pioneers, and of treasurers, to fit Cyrus and his armies for this great service.

Secondly, in case that all these three particular promises should not be enough to steal the hearts of the Jews to set on this hard work, and to hold out in it; the Lord in the next place, proclaims all his great attributes before them to encourage them in their way.

So when he was to put Moses on that great design of bringing the people of Israel out of Egypt, He proclaimed His name before him, Exodus 3:14, "I am that I am, thus shall thou say unto the children of Israel, *I am* hath sent me unto you." The line in Exodus 6:3 where he tells him of his great Name *Jehovah,* by which he says, "I was not known unto Abraham, Isaac, and Jacob," this head of the chapter runs onward from the end of verse 4 to verse 14. It is one continued, loud, large proclamation of the Lord's excellencies and royal prerogatives, by it to support their spirits against all difficulties. The sum of the whole encouragement may be rendered this way, "I can, God says, and I will muster and command all things from the rising of the sun and from the west," verse 5 and 6, "both light and darkness," verse 7, "the heavens, the skies, the earth," verse 8. "All these will I muster and draw forth for this work, rather than it shall die in the birth. And as for that pothead, that clay, Babylon, it shall here in know my love unto Israel," verse 9, "and shall feel what it is for a creature to strive with its Creator, or for a birth to tax those parents that begat and bare it," verse 10. This part reaches to verse 14.

The remainder, which is the third piece of the chapter, is a kind of twisted promise, partly respecting the deliverance from Babylon in the letter, and partly (according to the usual manner of the prophets) interweaving some passages concerning Christ and spiritual redemption, in the mystery.

The words of my text, if you look on them with reference to the bordering verses, they are an abrupt apostrophe. If you view them in themselves without that reference, they are an *epanorthosis* or correction.

First look on them with reference to the bordering verses; so you shall find that this verse of my text does not seem at all to be the same to other parts of the chapter. The whole series stands this way; the church having heard and considered all the promises, prophecies and passages of this strange work of salvation and redemption from Babylon, how that it shall be done by Cyrus, a heathen king, and enemy to the Jews. And observing also that there were so many crooked places that must be made straight, so many gates of brass that must be shattered and broken in pieces, verse 2, and having further considered, verse 8, that this same righteousness must drop down from heaven above, as it were by a miracle. It must come up from the earth beneath, as if it were from low and contemptible means. No, finally they having also seriously pondered that this grand redemption shall be done without price and without rewards, as verse 13, and who will do a work without wages? Who goes to war at his own costs? Yet says God, "he shall build my city and he shall let go my captives, not for price, nor rewards, says the Lords of hosts." Having considered all these strange circumstances and rubs in the way, all these meanders, these up hills and down hills in the passage; and having lain them together, she cries out like one astonished, and in a kind of abrupt apostrophe interrupts the prophet in his sermon with this mixed admiration twist fear and faith. The Scriptures say, "Verily thou art a God that hides thyself, O God of Israel the Savior," that is, while You hide Thyself, O God, yet You are the Savior of Israel.

So with reference to the bordering verses, the text is an abrupt interrupting apostrophe.

Next, consider the words in themselves, and they are a kind of *epanorthosis*, a correction. For in the former part of the verse, the church seemed to trip, stumble, and stagger, at the strangest of the manner of the prophesied deliverance from Babylon. It is carried on in such an abstruse, intricate, unusual way and method, that she cries out as one at a loss, (*verily thou art a God that hides thyself*). Here is her trip, her stagger, her stumble at the strange manner in the former part. But then she recovers herself again in the latter part to a confident persuasion of an undoubted good issue or end at last, concluding certainly that the upshot will be wonderful salvation to the Israel of God, though the manner is strange and various. The issue will be, shall be good and certain. "Though thou be (*she says*) a God that hides thyself, yet O God, I believe thou wilt be the Savior of Israel." So she trips in the first, and recovers herself in the latter, and you know the proverbs, *he that stumbles and does not fall, makes more speed in his way.* This is the state of the text. So that the former part of it is a kind of musing admiration at the strange manner of God's proceeding; the latter part is a confident persuasion of the final good issue.

If I would be curious to mince a text, both those general parts might admit of a more particular anatomy. As first in that strange hidden manner of this work, there are three several steps or degrees, and as many more (answerable to them) are to be found in the certain believed issue of this salvation.

In the manner is implied,

1. An obscurity; he is a *hidden* God.

2. The willingness of that obscurity, a *self-*hiding God.

3. The certainty of both, *verily thou art such a God.*
In this issue, there is an exact opposition to all those three, both in quantity and quality.

1. For this hidden God was not withstanding the God of Israel.

2. This self-hiding God was even during that time a Savior.

3. And the certainty, expressed in the asseveration verily is answered and overpowered by an admiration, in the interjection "O!" as though the mouth of the speaker had been too narrow for his heart and observation.

And so the whole tenor of the text does run somewhat like the beginning of Psalm 73:1, "Truly or yet God is good to Israel, even to such as are of a clean heart." Why truly or yet? See the next verse, verse 2, "but as for me my feet were almost gone, my steps had well-nigh flipped." Where we find in verse 3, "for I was envious at the foolish when I saw the prosperity of the wicked." Note here, he recovered himself in the issue, though he stumbled at the entrance. It seems that the Lord's dispensations in those days went on like this deliverance from Babylon; and this deliverance went on just (I think) like the motions of a clock. Fix your eyes steadfastly on a clock while it is going, you shall only hear and see the balance moving and clacking above but you cannot perceive the poises making any motion that while, neither can you discern the finger of the watch to go forwards; but take off your eye for a while, leaving a mark on the place, and then you shall find easily. In fact, when the clock has gone through an hour, you could not *perceive* it in motion. Such was the manner of this work. While the people of God steadfastly and continually fixed their eyes on it, it was advanced in such an abstruse, intricate and insensible way, that they could see no motion at all. So we read in Ezra 4:24, "Then ceased the work of the house of God which is at Jerusalem;" and yet even then it scarcely ceased, for in the next chapter, chapter 5 the prophets prophesied, verse 1, "And the eminent men begun to build again," verse 2 and 5. The balance of the clock continued their clack, and at last the clock struck out.

PART 2: THE DOCTRINE

So much ought necessarily to be said for draining, leveling and trenching the ground for a foundation. Now, not to detain you any longer from the thing that I principality intend, the observation from the whole text and context briefly explained, divided, debated and must run this way:

DOCTRINE: That God's great salvation of his people, but especially from Babylon, are commonly carried on in a mystery.

Observe this – here we find salvation *because* of a Savior. And it is so great a salvation, that it strikes the beholding church or prophet into an admiration they cannot express it without an interjection, "O God of Israel the Savior." And that this salvation is from Babylon, the whole tenor, grain and strain of the history declares.

Salvation is nothing else but the putting of a thing into a safe condition; and it is sometimes taken actively with respect to the author; as Exodus 14:13, "Stand still and see the salvation of God;" and so I say here, *the Lord's salvation*. Sometimes salvation is taken passively, with respect to the receiver; as you may read in the psalmist, Psalms 14:7, "O that the salvation of Israel was come out of Zion;" and so I say, the Lord's salvation of his people. Therefore both those significations are in the position; and both those sorts may be further considered, first, with respect to their subject whether as common, public, or general, respecting a whole nation, church or people; or as particular, private or special, of a place, member, or person.

Next, with respect to the object, or *material circa quam*. So there is a salvation in *spiritualibus and ecclesiasticis,* a spiritual, a religious salvation that is the same with reformation. And there is a salvation in *politicis, civilibus and secularibus,* a salvation in politic things, and this is the same with deliverance. In this place you must take in both, reformation and deliverance, because both are expressed in this prophecy, as we may gather out of Ezra 44:28, "Saying to Jerusalem, thou shall be built;" there is the civil or politic salvation, the state salvation, the deliverance. And to the temple, thy foundation shall be laid; there is the spiritual and ecclesiastical salvation, the church salvation, which is the reformation.

And accordingly I shall carry on my doctrine, both in the demonstrative and applicative parts of it, using the word *salvation* in both these acceptations, for reformation and deliverance. And so God's great salvations of his people, especially from Babylon, are carried on in a mystery.

Babylon in scripture is of two forts.

First, there is literal, eastern, Asiatic Babylon. This was the metropolis of Chaldea and sometimes of the world. Of this we read commonly in the Old Testament, and it is meant immediately in the text.

Next, there is mystical, western, European Babylon, this is *Rome*, the metropolis of Italy, and it was sometimes the Queen of the Nations. We read of it commonly in the New Testament. This is also included in the doctrine.

In a mystery, the Greek is a μυστήριον *musterion*, and for the smoother sounding μυστήριον signifies a *hidden, abstruse, and secret matter*; a thing shut up under bars and locks from common sense and carnal reason. It includes the following two conditions.

First, (*respectu Dei*) in respect of God, it is an act or work not of his common, general, ordinary providence; but of his particular, special, extraordinary power, wisdom, justice and mercy; it is not only the work of his hands, but of his finger; as the Egyptian-Magicians acknowledged concerning the plague of lice (Exodus 8:18-19) when they saw that there enchantments failed them in that particular, they said to Pharaoh, "this is the finger of the Lord." So in respect of the Lord, a mysterious carriage of a business it is (as Isaiah says elsewhere, chapter 28 verse 21). It is his work, his *strange* work, and his act, his *strange* act.

Next, (*respect nostri*) in respect of us men, it is hard to be understood, it is to the common multitude as a thing locked up in a strange language, as 1 Corinthians 14:2, I may allude at least, "for he that speaks in an unknown tongue, speaks not unto men, but unto God, for no man understands or hears him how it is in the spirit he speaks mysteries." In short, a mystery is to the generality of men, a paradox, a riddle, a secret that requires a revelation; as Daniel 2:28, "There is a God in Heaven that reveals secrets," says the Septuagint.[1]

So much I mean by a mysterious carriage in general, *viz.* when a salvation is wrought out in a course,

---

[1] The Septuagint is the Greek translation of the Hebrew Old Testament.

besides, beyond, or against, the beaten rode of common providence and carnal capacities. Let us borrow but one more verse to express it allusively. See Proverbs 30:18, "There be three things which are too wonderful for me, yea four which I know not." Read verse 19, "The way of an eagle in the air, the way of a serpent upon a rock, and the way of a ship in the middle of the sea." Just such is usually the way of the Lord in carrying on his great salvations, and especially from Babylon. Let us severally consider those three comparisons.

The way of an eagle in the air. Among all the elements, the air alone is invisible and least palpable; it most easily gives a passage to any natural body, and as suddenly comes together again. Among all fowls of the heaven, the eagle is accounted strongest, and therefore flies very swiftly; and being a bird of prey, her motion is exceedingly various too, according to the course of the game that is before her. Who then can guess before, or trace out afterwards, the way of an eagle in the air?

The way of a serpent upon a rock, is no less hidden. Oh! How does this creeping creature wind, wave and weave it as she goes? What self-obliterating chiverdils and indentures are made in her motion? Now the head points this way, in a moment it stands to the other side; it is hard for him that meets her, to guess whether or not she is coming towards him. But especially when a serpent goes on a rock then there is no means to hear her motion as in the sand and among the leaves, or to see and trace it as in the dust and clay; no noise, no impression is made to help the ear or eye of him that seeks her way. But then there is a ship next.

But *the way of the ship in the middle of the sea*, is more abstruse and uncertain then both the former. There are three principles of variation and uncertainty in her motion. First, the wind above, that blows *where it wills, and we hear the sound of it but do not know where it comes, nor where it goes.* Next, the waters beneath are the most inconstant of elements; for (besides that they are driven of fierce winds) their own natural ebbing and flowing, are a daily constant against inconstancy.

But lastly, the greatest principle of uncertainty, is the mind and pleasure of her pilot within, who at his will often turns her to half a point against the motions both of winds and waters. In short, she finds no path before her, she leaves no tract behind her, and all her moves, above, beneath, within, are most uncertain. Who then can know the way of a ship in the middle of the sea? So, not to be guessed, not to be traced are the Lord's carriages of these kinds of salvation.

My doctrine is somewhat like that piece of Ezekiel's wheel, which he calls *rotarn in rota* Ezekiel 1:16, "...their appearance and their work were as it were a wheel in the middle of a wheel." So here is a doctrine in the middle of a doctrine. The first is as it were the general thesis concerning God's great salvations indefinitely. The second is as a hypothesis drawn out of the womb of that thesis, concerning the redemption from Babylon in particular. And accordingly I shall have an eye distinctly both in my demonstrative and applicative parts, looking on these two, severely and apart.

First then demonstratively, the doctrine is concerning the general thesis, *that God's great salvations of his people, are commonly carried on in a mystery.* O what rare maps of saving wonders, what admirable anatomies of public mercies could I hear spread before your eyes this day! Only let us crop off some full ears.

Jacob and his Sons

Observe first that great preservation of old Jacob and his family by their removal from Canaan in Egypt, in the time of the famine. How strangely was that deliverance brought about! The design was to preserve Jacob and his posterity, and to make a way for that great work or redemption out of Egypt which followed after. But mark the method; first Joseph, who by his own dreams and his father's hopes was to be the glory and prop of the family, he must be given for lost to his father, his brethren, himself. His father believes he was torn in pieces, his brethren sell him into Egypt for a bond slave, and there he is cast into prison by Potiphar after he had been first advanced. So that now not only the father's hopes are dead and buried, but Joseph's own faith is put to the trial; and all this to make way for the *greater* deliverance. Do not these things now look like a salvation? No further yet, old Jacob must be necessitated by famine to send his children down into Egypt to buy food, and there he must first lose his son Simeon; and next his dearest Benjamin must be sent and lost in his own and brethren's apprehensions. And yet all this appears at last to be nothing else but a mere plot of mercy, a very ambush of providence for the greater advantage and advancement of the whole family, as you see in the narrative. For, first all the brethren of Joseph with their household had by this their preservation and preferment where otherwise they would have perished by famine. Secondly, Benjamin who was the most hazarded and lost man among them since the cup was found in his sack; he had gotten a multiplied portion. Thirdly, Jacob himself (the father) he gains five sons for one, that is, for his dear Joseph, whom he conceived to be lost, he receives the same Joseph again with an addition of Ephraim and Manasseh; and also two of his own sons whom he conceived to be lost, (Simeon and Benjamin), are cast in to boot. So five are returned for one. This was an ambush of mercy by God. And finally as for Joseph himself, he must have a double blessing and portion, and is made the head of two tribes; one of which (Ephraim) in short time after the throne was erected, got away ten of the twelve tribes from the scepter of Judah. Was not this a *mystery* of mysteries? So far concerning the salvation of Jacob and his family when they were carried from Canaan into Egypt.

Moses

But in the next place, the preservation of the seed of Jacob in Egypt, and their return from there to Canaan again, at the end of four hundred and thirty years, was more admirable then their first going there, their strange preservation in Egypt was shadowed in that emblem of a fiery bush not consumed, Exodus 3:2 and the angel of the Lord appeared to Moses in a flame of fire out of the midst of a bush. This was a token of Israel's continuance in the midst of the iron fiery furnace. Their salvation or deliverance was in this manner. Moses, not while he was in favor in Pharaoh's court, but after that he was a fugitive, and exile being a stammering shepherd, must be the principal instrument in the work; and he together with his brother Aaron, (another contemptible Levite) with a rod in their hands, must fetch out of Egypt in spite of a hardened King, and all his magicians, (how many do you guess there were?) and save a hundred thousand men, besides a mix multitude with women and children. He that can deny this to be a heap, a cluster of wonders or chance happenings, he should be recorded as a wonder of great stupidity.

Gideon the Judge

Once more, a third instance, in the time of the Judges; see but that great salvation and deliverance of Israel out of the hand of the Midianites and their confederates; and let us cast our eye equally on both parties, the oppressors and the delivered. First, look on the oppressors; consider their power, their cruelty. In Judges 6 in the first verse you shall read that Israel had served an apprentice of seven years under their tyranny. In the second, third, fourth, and fifth verses, you shall read, that poor Israel was sane to run into dens of the mountains, and caves, and strongholds, that their fruits were destroyed as soon as they came forth; that their enemies came up as grasshoppers, and left no sustenance for Israel, neither sheep, nor ox, nor ass; and this fury still increased, for verse 5 they came up with their cattle and their tents, and they came as grasshoppers for multitude, for both they and their camels were without number. That for the enemies' part. Next, look on Israel *the delivered*, and consider their power and strength. Their general, would you know what he was? He was Gideon, a thresher, afterward called Jerubbaal, a man called away from the barn, from the "threshing floor," Judges 6:16. His family was poor in Manasseh, and he was the least in that poor family; a man taken from the very flail to be a *captain general*. And for his forces, it is true, at the first they were a considerable number; they were (the text says) two and thirty thousands; but then the Lord falls to lessening of them. First, he begins with a proclamation, and on this some two and twenty thousand of them to go away. Next, the Lord has another experiment, of lapping, and by that means he sends away all the remaining ten thousand, except only poor three hundred; so that now about the hundredth part of Gideon's forces is left. This handful under the command of Gideon the thresher must go against the numberless Midianites. But yet a handful with choice weapons, at some advantages, may do great things. True, but in the next place look on their arms, both defensive and offensive, Judges 7:20, they were to go with empty pitchers, and lamps within the pitchers in one hand, and in the other hand they must hold a trumpet, and with blowing those trumpets, breaking the pitchers, and holding out the lamps, they shall beat the Midianites. Here is a mystery with a witness; a numberless army, totally routed and cut in pieces without any weapon appearing against them, broken in pieces with the breaking of pitchers, frightened with the sight of lamps, and utterly blown away by the sound of trumpets. This is God's great salvation carried on in a mystery.

Salvation from Babylon

Yea, but what is all this to salvation from Babylon?

That I confess is the hypothesis, and may as strangely and fully be shown and proved as the general; even that God's salvations from Babylon are carried on in a mystery. There are two Babylon's mentioned in scripture. First, Babylon the Eastern, which was that in Chaldea, the literal A Babylon; and Babylon the Western, which is that in Italy, Rome, the mystical Babylon. Concerning both these, I could show you distinctly that God's great salvations out of them are commonly carried on in a mystery.

First, concerning salvation and redemption out of the hand of literal, Eastern, Chaldean Babylon, we find no less than four whole books of the scriptures spent to show the extraordinary deliverances of God's people from there. Two of these books are historical, as Ezra and Nehemiah; other two are prophetical, as Haggai and Zechariah. It would be too long for me to epitomize all the expressions of those books, and of some others, which show the wonderful mysterious carriage of that work. Only take notice of two places to this purpose.

The Visions of Ezekiel

First, of that vision of Ezekiel, which, as I conceive, typifies the Jewish return from Babylon, Ezekiel 1. The whole vision is large, in it there is mention of a whirl wind out of the North, a great cloud, a self-enfolding fire, and out of the midst of it the color of amber, verse 4. Also out of the same midst, the likeness of "four living creatures," like men, verse 5, they had four faces, four wings, they had the feet of calves, the hands of men, verse 6 and 7. Strange mixtures and varieties! I will only mention on that piece which concerns the wheels.

Those wheels (as interpreters conceive) signify the Lord's *providence*. And the motions of the wheels, the several acts and turnings of that providence in the deliverance of his people from Babylon the Eastern. Therefore, verse 18, it is said the wheels were "full of eyes round about;" the eyes of the Lord do run through the world, but I would especially take notice there of the *involucra providentie*, the intricate involutions and encircling of those wheels. It is set down, verse 16. Their work was, as it were a wheel in the middle of a wheel, to signify, the eccentrically and concentrically motions of that people's return from Babylon, where Ezekiel was now a captive among them, as you may read in verse 1.

The Prophecy of Zechariah

But a more full and clear place to show the mysteriousness of the deliverance of Israel from Babylon the Eastern, is that in the prophecy of Zechariah. Look on that one text in chapter 1 verse 8. "I saw by nights, and behold a man riding upon a red horse, and am stood among the myrtle trees that were in the bottom, and behind him were these red horses, speckled and white."

This man is *Christ*; these horses with him are his angels; and their design is to bring the Jews out of Babylon the Eastern, where they had remained under God's indignation these threescore and ten years, as you may read, verse 12. But mark how that redemption is carried in the clouds; there are no less than five notes of obscurity in that verse, signifying the mysterious progress of the work.

1. It is said that this vision was in the "night" both in the night (that is) of *adversity*, and in the night of *ignorance*. There was little comfort, few prophets were left to revive or direct them.

2. This man is in "a bottom" that is, obscurely placed out of sight. And as if that were not enough;

3. In this bottom he stood among the "myrtle trees," there was a grove of tall trees, in the center of a valley; so that the Jews might well have said to him as here in the test, *verily though art a God that hides thy self*. But that is not all.

4. His forces, his auxiliaries, stood "behind" him, says the text, that is, they were not only covered by the valley and the myrtle trees, but they were covered by the interposition of Christ's person too; they were trebly

covered, with the valley, with the myrtle trees, and with Christ that stood before them.

5. And this "speckling" or dappling of the horses is observable, it shows the interchangeable, partly colored texture of that work; yes the red and the white with the speckled, show the mixture of peace and blood that they trooped together in this work.

But here some might object, *true, true, all this is confessed, that great salvations in general, and in special those from Eastern Babylon have sin, are carried on in a mystery; but now such wonders and miracles do cease; what is all this to do with us in these times?*

Daniel's Vision

In the next place therefore, I will show that salvation from Babylon the Western, from Romish Babylon, that is, the salvation we are now on, must also be carried on in a mystery.

For this purpose, first I would commend to you a choice text for our times, I think it is as a word on the wheels in there our days, until Daniel 2 where you have a prophetic vision, a vision of an image, whose head is of gold, the breast and arms of silver, the belly and thighs of brass, the legs of iron, and the feet part iron and part clay. Expositors conceive that this fourfold image signifies the four famous monarchies of the world: the Assyrian, the Persian (as it is commonly called), the Grecian, and the Roman monarchies. The first three of these are past, and (without question) we have come now to the lower part of the fourth. I mean the Roman Empire is removed, and we see the mixture of iron and clay, whether you take the iron and clay for the division of the Roman Empire into the Western and Eastern according to verse 42. And as the toes of the feet were part of iron and part of clay, so the Kingdoms shall be partly strong, and partly broken, (or brittle); the Eastern Empire was first broken off; or whether you will understand a kind of compounding of succession between the Roman and German Empires. Or whether (lastly) a mingling and dawbing of the spiritual and temporal, that is, the imperial and papal powers together; yet still, we have come to the feet of the image, and to the very toes of those feet, which are this Babylon the Western in its present condition; for both branches of the proper Roman Empire are withered, and the

German eagle was never so striped of her plumes as now. Yes, the very papacy of late sheds her prelatic feathers continually. So that both scripture chronologies, and common sense, evidence that the image stands at best but on tip toe; and the time is at hand, (I conceive it is present) in which it shall be thrown down and utterly abolished. But you will ask me, *how must it be thrown down? By what means shall God's people be delivered out of the hands of this Roman Babylon?* Truly by as strange means as ever was read of; see the 34th and 44th verses of the chapter. First in the 34th verse "Thou sawest till that a stone was cut out without hands." Here is a mystery, a stone cut out without hands, or which was not in hand, which struck the image on his feet which were of iron and clay, and broke them to pieces. This stone is Jesus Christ, (as Matthew 21:42). "The stone which the builders rejected, the same is become the head of the corner," (verse 44), "and whosoever shall fall on this stone, shall be broken, but on whomsoever it shall fall, it will grind him to powder." This scripture is most exactly true concerning Christ's governing in his church and he will crush all oppositions to the potter's vessels. Again, this stone is cut out of the mountain without hands. That is, the image shall be cast down, and the kingdom of Christ shall be set up, not by common carnal might and means, but in a special and *divine* manner, for so it followed in Daniel's interpretation (verse 44 and 45). In the days of these kings (at the close of the last empire) shall the God of heaven set up a kingdom which "shall never be destroyed," and the kingdom shall not be left to other people, but is shall break in pieces and consume all these kingdoms, and it shall stand forever. For you saw that the stone was cut out of the mountain without hands, and that it broke in pieces the iron, the brass, the clay, the silver, and the gold. The great God has made known to the king what shall come to pass hereafter. I could with that this seasonable place of Daniel might come often into the thoughts of all our serious active spirits in these times for their encouragement. But rather, because I find that the Jesuits themselves fall in with my present interpretation, so far, that they have much to do to make such a retreat as may seem to excuse the Pope and Rome from the names of *antichrist* and *Babylon*. Another vision of the four monarchies that are the same as this, is to be seen in Daniel 7.

The Revelation

Add to these, that place of the apocalypse (which is, as it were, the book of Daniel in the New Testament) Revelation 14:6-8, there is shown that the salvation of God's people from Babylon the mystical, shall be carried on in a mystery, verse 6. "And I saw another angel fly in the midst of heaven, having the everlasting gospel to preach unto them that dwell on the earth," verse 7, "saying with a loud voice, fear God and give glory to Him, for the hour of his judgment is come." Here on the eighth verse, there flowed another angel, saying, "Babylon is fallen, is fallen, that great city." Fallen? Why, what ailed her? What was it that threw her down? Surely it was nothing but that the angel flew in the midst of heaven, having an everlasting gospel to preach to them that dwell on the earth. It was merely the *preaching of the gospel*, if you will know it. So that it seems the Lord will throw down Babylon the mystical, just as he threw down the walls of Jericho, with a holy blast, by the breath of the gospel; it shall be preached flat to the ground. It is no marvel that our prelates were so angry with lecturers.

Another expression of her overthrow might be gathered out of Revelation 17:13-16. I will but name it, because my reverend brother already preached on it in the morning and has prevented me. And chapter 18:2 where you shall find that Babylon shall be thrown down merely by God's immediate supernatural working on the spirits of those men that were formerly friends and factors for the whore. For first it said, verse 13 that, these (that is, the ten horns, which are 10 kings) have one mind, and shall give their power and strength to the beast, verse 14. These shall make war with the lamb. Here they untie and agree well enough to persecute the saints. But read on to verse 16. There they fall on the whore their late mother and mistress; the ten horns which you saw, these shall hate the whore, and make her desolate and naked, and shall eat her flesh and burn her with fire. A strange alteration indeed! But how could such near friends fall in to such bitter enmity so suddenly? No cause at all but this, verse 17, for God has put into their hearts, both to unite and fall off again.

So you see not only God's great salvations of his people in general, but especially those from Babylon, are to be carried on in a *mystery*.

But is it not strange that the Lord delights this way to obscure and hide himself in the carriage of his great works? Would it not do better (according to our judgments and apprehensions) if they were carried on in the common rode of ordinary providence, so that every man might see them before him while they are doing, as well as behind him, when they are done?

I answer, the nature of man is apt to reason this way, as Job 13:3 and Jeremiah 12:1 did. And I could answer such questions with St. Paul's, *O homo tu qui*, Romans 9:20. "Nay but, O man, who art thou that repliest against God? Shall the thing formed say to him that formed it, Why hast thou made me thus?" But that I may satisfy, as well as confute, I shall add, that there are reasons to show that it is not only fit, but necessary, yes, triply necessary, that such great salvations (especially from Babylon) should be mysteriously carried on.

It is necessary,

1. For the Lord's greater glory.

2. For his people's greater good.

3. For his enemies' greater confusion.

First, the Lord hides himself in this way while he is saving, for *his own greater glory*. There is a clear and full place to this particular, Proverbs 25:2. "It is the glory of God to conceal a thing, but the honor of king's is to search out a matter," *rem abscondere*, that is, so to hide both himself and his work, that men may not be able beforehand to guess at him where he will go next; nor yet to trace after him, when he is gone before. The latter expression, namely, (that no man might go after him) is to be found in Ecclesiastes 7:13-14, "Consider the work of God, for who can make that straight, which he has made crooked?" And verse 14, "In the day of prosperity be joyful, but in the day of adversity consider; God also has set the one over against the other, to the end that man should find nothing after him." Note this, (God has set the one over against the other, to the end that man should find nothing after him) that is, the Lord incubates his works, he intricately and (to our apprehension) promiscuously mingles the acts and effects of his common providence, he traverses his ground, he goes on, as it were, by jumps, that so the mind of man may not be able to tract and follow him, but may sit down admiring the depths of his wisdom, and the strength of his power.

He leaves so much print of his footsteps as to convince the atheist, that he went that way, and yet so little as to puzzle the naturalist to find out the manner of his going.

All that God does is abundantly for the Lord's glory in all his attributes to conceal a matter. Every common painter is able to paint a plain piece of work, (*simulare cupressum*) as the proverb is; to paint a tree or a bough, but he is an artist indeed that is able to draw forth a shadowed piece. Every indifferent good soldier is able to fight *pell-mell*, or on a party, hand to hand; but he is the skillful man that is able to order an ambush that can manage *a stratagem*. Believe it brethren, therefore does the Lord draws his salvations in shadowed works that you may see the depth of his wisdom; therefore the Lord uses to overcome by ambushes, so the glory of his grace to his people, and the glory of his wisdom even among his enemies, may be greatly seen. That is the first ground, for his own greater glory.

The second ground why he carries his work in a mystery, is for the greater good of his people. You have only to choose a place to this purpose in the book of Deuteronomy, that alone may suffice, Deuteronomy 8 beginning at verse 2. "And though shall remember all the way which the Lord thy God led thee these forty years in the wilderness, to humble thee, and to prove thee, to know what was in your heart, whether thou would keep his commandments or not; and he humbled thee, and suffered thee to hunger, and fed thee with manna, which though new not, neither did they fathers know, that he might make thee know, that man does not live by bread alone, but by every word that proceeds out of the mouth of the Lord does man live. Thy garment waxed not old upon thee, neither did thy feet swell these forty years." God could have carried on Israel in a shorter time and in a direct way, not in such a maze and labyrinth through the wilderness forty years together; he could have carried them through within forty months. He could have fed them from the earth if it had pleased him, and could have preserved them so as they should never have been strained for lack of provision, so as that the water should never have been scant or bitter. Yes, he could have made it where they should never have met with an enemy; these and all other hardships the Lord could have prevented. But he did purposely suffer these intricate abstruse difficulties to fall in, for the proving of his people, for so it follows in the 16th verse of the same chapter, "He fed thee with manna in the wilderness, which thy fathers knew not, that he might humble thee, and that he might prove thee." Not but that he knew their hearts, but because they did not know their own hearts, much less did others know their spirits. Alas how few of us know our own hearts while we lived in peace and prosperity in our countries and callings, until the Lord by the intricateness of these means, and by the mazes of his proceedings pumped up and drew forth our inward parts by regeneration! So humbling, proving, improving and engaging, were the Lord's four grand designs on Israel. And on the same grounds did he lead Abraham, Isaac, Jacob and Joseph at their first calling in a strange country, by extraordinary providence, to prove, and improve their graces. Yes, and to feed them in a specific manner spiritually speaking (as it were) for greater mercies and services. And I am persuaded that by that time God has brought together both ends of this mysterious salvation that he is now working, every serious Christian among us shall be able to say, that he could not have been without any one of all those obstructions and afflictions that we have met with. No, I am persuaded that we shall all freely conclude at last, that if we had not lost all, we would have been undone; if we had not been plundered, we had been begged; if all these mysterious abstruse difficulties had not fallen in, we never had seen half so much of God, of ourselves, of grace, or sin, reformation, as I hope we shall now discern. But I hasten to the third point.

A third ground, why God delights in this way to carry on his great salvations; and especially, his Babylon's redemption, is for the enemy's greater confusion, either of their faces, or persons.

First, for the greater confusion of their faces, when God having put them in hope of winning the day, shall outreach and out do them at last; when the Lord shall so befool them, that in the conclusion they shall see themselves wiped out of all their hopes, this will be abundantly for their greater shame and confusion of face. When an oraculous Achitophel shall find his counsel over reached by a plain Hushai, that is the next way to make him become his own hangman. When an insolent Haman shall see himself degraded by a modest godly female Esther, it is the way to make him fall down on the bed, and almost to wish himself dispatched on his own death. When a Sisera, a triumphant Sisera, shall be nailed to the ground by the hand of a Jew. When a Pharaoh and a Herod shall be beaten and eaten with lice, so that they shall be sane to stand shrugging and picking like a beggar in a bush, oh what confusion of face must this necessarily be, not only on the persons themselves that so miscarry, but on all their tribe and adherents? What gross confusion of face (we could guess with ourselves) was there to Sanballat, Tobiah, Geshem and the rest, when after all their secret fraud and open force, after all their letters and machinations to hinder the building of the temple, yet the work was perfected at last? You shall read in Nehemiah (Chapter 6:15) that the wall was finished in the 25th day of the month Elul in fifty and two days, so that all their plans, charge and diligence came short; everything to them was lost. There on, in the 16h verse, says the text, "it came to pass that when all our enemies heard thereof, and all the heathen that were about us saw these things, they were much cast down in their own eyes," that is, they do not know which way to look, nor where to bestow their faces, but stood like so many thieves taken in the very act, casting their eyes towards the ground.

O! do but guess with yourselves, honorable and beloved, when God shall bring about this present mysterious work of his salvation, and put a glorious issue to it, (for this work must have a glorious issue) I say it again in short, when at the end of these troubles the worldly and wicked politicians shall find themselves outwitted, the potentates overpowered, and the wealthy men out-pursed, and that all this shall be done by those whom they accounted mere foolishness, weakness, and poverty; then, guess with yourselves how will the most active, industrious and impudent enemies be able to lift up their foreheads? How will they look on one another? Surely just like a kennel of hungry dogs that always have been hotly pursuing their prey or game, and at night have missed and lost it in the woods. I cannot but think with myself that it will be worth all the pains and cost that an active man shall lay out in this work, but to see that Babel, that confusion of tongues and faces, that will befall the enemies at last. A shadow of this confusion of face and language you find prophesied in Revelation 18:15-17, "The merchants which were made rich by her, shall stand far off, weeping and wailing, and saying, alas, alas, that great city that was clothed in fine linen, and purple, and scarlet, and decked with gold and precious stones, and pearls, for in one hour so great riches is come to nothing." And verse 19. "They," that is, the kings of the earth, the merchants, the ship masters, and sailors, "cast dust on their heads and cried, weeping and wailing, saying, alas, alas, that great city wherein were made rich all that had ships in the sea by reason of her costliness, for in one hour she is made desolate." So God does it for the greater confusion of the faces of his enemies.

Or, secondly, if they lack so much modestly as to be capable of confusion of face, yet these hidden carriages shall work for the greater confusion of their persons. They shall be the more utterly confounded by these mysteries. If the men of the old world will be so impudently wicked, as not to blush at Noah's preaching and building , they shall wade knee deep in the flood to beg admission into the ark, but not obtain it. If the king of Egypt and all his gypsies will be so shameless as to dodge ten times with the Lord, they shall at last cry and fly against the returning seas, and all in vain, Exodus 14:26, so that all the meanders and intricate carriages of the work until then, did but ripen them for greater personal confusion. Had Pharaoh come in on the first summons (the first miracle) or on the second or third, the man might have saved his life, and perchance his kingdom; but therefore the Lord will suffer him to be baited on with a kind of vicissitude of losses and victories, that all this might harden his heart, and the hearts of all his magicians, desperately to plunge themselves into the bottom of the sea, where they might be slain and buried at once.

This very ground (for the enemy's greater destruction) is hinted in this same prophecy of Ezra 44:25 he says, "He frustrates the tokens of the liars, and makes diviners mad; he turns wise men backward, and makes their knowledge foolish." Mark this passage here, he carries his work so mysteriously, that he might frustrate the tokens of the liars, that is, of those that were so confident on some poor petty successes and victories which they had obtained against the people of God, that (on this) they dare to divine, and promise to their party a total, final and speedy conquest. Now when God shall turn everything about again, in a time, in a way, where they did not look for it, doubtless such a strange surprise will put them into the condition of the men of Ai when they were encompassed by Joshua's *stratagem*, Joshua

8:20, "They had no power to flee this way or that way," verse 22, "they were in the midst of Israel, some on this side, and some on that side, and they smote them so that they let none of them remain or escape." And all this was done by a stratagem, for before in verse 15, Joshua and all Israel made as if they were beaten before them (of Ai) and fled by the way of the wilderness.

So you see it is a necessary and rational truth that the Lord this way carries on his great salvations, viz. for his own greater glory, for his people's greater benefit, and for his enemy's greater confusion. Therefore it is not out of lack either of power or wisdom, but out of a transcendence of both that he orders his deliverances in such a manner. So much may demonstrate the thesis or general part.

But, secondly, if you demand a particular reason for the hypothesis, viz. why salvations from Babylon are also carried in a mystery? I answer, that there is a special ground for this branch also. And it is this in short.

Our Babylon (I mean the Western) was raised in a mystery, and therefore it is good reason that it should be thrown down in the same manner. In 2 Thessalonians

2:6, "You shall find that Babylon is built up in a mystery...The mystery of iniquity does already work."

That noble Frenchman throughout this mystery of iniquity, gives us a sufficient commentary on this text, by discovering the parts of that mystery, showing the pedigree of antichrist, and how he has gathered his stolen feathers together, of which when every bird shall take his own, he shall be left naked and bare.

Also in Revelation 17:4-6 you shall see that Babylon was *raised* in a mystery. "And the woman was arrayed in purple and scarlet color and decked with gold and precious stones, having a golden cup in her hand, full of abominations and filthiness of her fornication." This woman is Rome, the Western Babylon. And on her forehead was a name written in capital letters, "Mystery, Babylon the great, the mother of harlots, and abominations of the earth." Called "mystery" because she was raised in a mystery; that is, she got up to her height insensibly, cunningly; her way in getting up was like the way of an eagle in the air, or like the way of a serpent on a stone, winding, and screwing itself onwards by degrees; untraceably; or as the way of a ship in the sea, which goes on swiftly when she seems to stand still. So Babylon was raised and built in a mystery, and therefore it is but just and proportional that she should be cast down and ruined in a mystery.

No, we have a hint, yes a prophetic command that this proportion shall be observed in the ruin and destruction of this Babylon in Revelation 18:6, "Reward her even as the she rewarded you, and double unto her double according to her works." And verse 7, how much she has glorified herself and lived deliciously, so much sorrow and torment give her; that is, let her be cast down by the same steps by which she climbed up, both for manner and measure.

So you see grounds for the general and also for the particular, why God's great salvations of his people and especially from Babylon, are, shall be, must be so mysteriously carried on. The application is the great errand in which I am sent at this time.

PART 3: APPLICATION

Why are the Lord's great salvations of his people especially from Babylon, carried on in a mystery? Then my first dose or portion is merely preparatory. Let us make English of this text, by enquiring and searching whether or not the present great work of salvation and reformation that is in your hands (for it is a work of salvation) is carried on in a mystery? What? Is it a plain work of common providence in which ordinary causes bring forth their wanted effects and issues, without any remarkable variation? Or rather, is it not an extraordinary, elaborate, shadowed masterpiece, altogether made up of stratagems, paradoxes, and wonders? If so, then comfort yourselves, you may conclude it will be a great salvation, yes (as I shall show) a salvation from Babylon. So then, the whole business of this preparatory use will be to enquire and inform ourselves distinctly and critically in this great question, "when is a salvation carried on in a mystery?" Or, *how may I know such* work?

I answer, as Psalm 111:2, "The works of the Lord are great; yet they may be sought out of all them that have pleasure therein." I shall endeavor for our direction and encouragement, in these trouble times, to give some special evidences of a *hiding savior* that is of a great, Babylon's, mysterious redemption.

1. First when the work is carried on spiritually. This I shall call *supra naturam* above nature.

2. When, casually, which is *preter naturam* besides nature.

3. When, contrarily and contradictorily *contra naturam* even against nature.

First when a work is carried on *supra naturam* (spiritually) that is, more by spiritual than by fleshly means. So we read of the Jewish redemption from Babylon, Zechariah 4:6, "Then he (*that is, the angel*) speaks and said, this is the word of the Lord unto Zerubbabel, saying, not by might, or arms, nor by power, but by my spirit says the Lord of Hosts." "Who art thou," verse 7, "O great mountain?" It was a mountain of rubbish that lay there (as some conceive) being the ruins of the former temple, as Nehemiah 4:2 and 10. This mountain must be removed here so the ground could be leveled for a foundation. But how shall this be done? "*Not by might, nor by power*, but he shall bring forth the corner stone thereof, which shouting, crying grace, grace unto it." It should be done without hands, only by the word of the Lord's mouth, as the earth and heavens were created. But in Haggai 4:14 you shall find a threefold stirring of spirits that carried on that work. "And the Lord stirred up the spirit of Zerubbabel (it was an immediate working on his spirit, which neither man nor devils are able to reach) the son of Shealtiel, governor of Judah; and the spirit of Joshua, the son of Josedech the high priest and the spirit of all the remnant of the people. God moved the spirit of the temporal rulers, of Zerubbabel," that is as it were the parliament; God moved the spirit of those of the church, of Joshua the high priest, and of Haggai, and Zechariah the prophets, as it were the Assembly of Divines; and God moved the spirit of all the remnant of the people (the whole commonalty) and they came and worked in the house of the Lord of Hosts their God. It seems it was not for wages or out of any constraint, but only because the Lord had touched their spirits and inclined their hearts to this service. So it is said of Cyrus in Ezra 1:1, "The Lord stirred up the spirits of Cyrus King of Persia, he gave the Jews leave to build, and did assist them, and supply them with necessaries for the service." And in chapter 5:1, the prophets, Haggai and Zechariah the son of Iddo, "prophesied unto the Jews that were in Judah and Jerusalem in the name of the God of Israel, even unto them." Then, verse 2, raised up "Zerubbabel the son of Shealtiel and Ieshua the son of Iozadek, and began to build the house of God." Why, what moved them at that time above another? Only the ministers preached to them about the work. As before I showed that the walls of Babylon must be preached down, so it seems here that the walls of the temple must be preached up. Haggai and Zachariah fell to preaching, and then the rulers and the people do fall to building.

How parallel is our case with this? Has might or weakness, flesh or spirit, (I ask of your own consciences) had the greatest stroke in our greatest salvations here? Have not the touched hearts, the willing spirits ever been the chief instruments? Is it not most evident that the Lord has touched some hearts with the spirit of wisdom and counsel, as sometimes he touched the heart of Bezaleel and Aholiah, filling them with his spirits, in knowledge to devise cunning works, to work in gold and in silver. Exodus 31:2, so among us has he not given an extraordinary spirit of counsel and wisdom into the hearts of men, even then when it was feared that disuse and oppression had quite worn out all the old race of true English hearts? Who had thought we had been so rich in parliamentary spirits, as appears this day?

Again, others have been as it were inspired with a spirit of courage and magnanimity beyond president, and even to their own admiration. Yes some like Gideon in the story before have been called off from mean employments, and yet have answered great expectations in the services of war. So that I cannot but guess that succeeding generations writing the history of these times will speak rather of a creation than of a generation of soldiers in our age.

Once more, how many nobles, gentry, ministers and people, everywhere are suddenly sprung up like Jonah's gourd against this hot season? Men accomplished with so many graces, gifts, qualifications, for this work, as if they had been inspired, but out and created purposely for this service? Believe it, these are things that deserve a most serious consideration, they prove that the work is carried on spiritually. But that is not all.

Secondly, salvation is then carried on in a mystery when it is carried on *praeter naturam*. In English it is "casually" or "accidentally;" that is, through a multitude of extraordinary accidents and casualties. By casualties I do not mean the acts or effects of pagan fortune, but the acts and effects of extraordinary and special *providence*; when there is a frequent confluence of such acts appearing in our salvations, this must necessarily be besides nature's rode; for *que casu siunt ea raro fiunt*, that is, casualties are rarities, the heathen says, or, things done by chance are seldom done. Now when we shall see such events fall in frequently, then we must conclude that he finger of God is there, this is not according to the common rule and rode of men.

That you may understand my meaning a little more fully in this particular, I will give you an instance of this confluence of casualties in the book and case of Esther, chapter 6. When Haman had made sure with King Ahasuerus (that is Xerxes) for the utter extirpation of the Jews, and that Esther had now begun mother mine to counter work him, see what a heap, what a cluster of seasonable casual circumstances happily fell in for the advantage of Esther, and the disadvantage of Haman. So we see this in short.

First, in verse 1, it is said that "on that night could not the king sleep." What night was that? Just the next night before that Esther stood engaged to break Mordecai's matter to the king on the next day, chapter 5 verse 8, "the very night before that day, the king could not sleep." And it was also just the night before that Haman meant to beg the execution of Mordecai. The night immediately before these two things were to be set on work, the king could not sleep. Why, what ailed him? We hear of no extraordinary sad tidings which were brought him that could hinder his sleep; we read of no distemper of body that lay on him; then doubtless God's hand was in it, therefore he could not sleep. But that is not all.

On this (secondly) he commanded to bring the book of records of the Chronicles to be read before him. True, we say reading and preaching will bring men to sleep though they have little disposition to it before. But all this could not incline him to slumber. This further shows the hand of God.

Well, thirdly, it was found written in the book, that Mordecai had done a choice piece of service for the king. Found, how was it found? How did it come to hand? Did the reader willingly turn to this place that so he might make way to ingratiate Mordecai? That is improbable, because Haman was now the darling of the court, and was Mordecai's known and protest enemy. Or, what did the king command that he should turn to that place? No, that is not probable either; because we find by the king's next question that he did not know to the contrary but that Mordecai had been already rewarded for this service. How then did this come about? Surely, that God directed the Eunuch when Philip joined himself to his chariot to be reading that place of Isaiah the prophet, Acts 8, and that voice that cried to Augustine, *tolle lege*, "take up and read," it seems that very providence did direct all this, that among all sorts of books the king should pitch on history, and among all sorts of history this volume, and among all the parts of this volume, this page, this passage, that so way might be made for Esther's intended motion.

Well, fourthly, verse 3, and the king said, "What honor and dignity has been done to Mordecai for this?" Why did the king take notice of this service at this time more than formerly; for it is said, chapter 2 verse 22 that Esther had (formerly) certified the king of this business in Mordecai's name, yet then no reward is on you? But it seems Mordecai's reward was kept for this very time by an act of *extraordinary providence*.

But fifthly (to put a heap of casualties together) that, Haman should so seasonably come in, in that very nick of time when Ahasuerus was studying how to reward Mordecai. That Haman should come in with that request and motion for the executing of Mordecai. Add to these, the king's admission of Haman, the question propounded to him, and Haman's answer to that question, all which you may read in chapter 6 verses 4-6. And then all these grains put together do make a great weight. Let all these causal circumstances be cast in, and you must confess that every particular of them being a several piece of wonder, the whole narrative makes up little less than *a miracle*.

Honorable and beloved, how easily could I show you the faces of such like casualties, or petty wonders, in the glass of your own proceedings? You have instances enough of your own (I mean in your own history) to parallel all these particulars and a thousand more; I do not need to go borrowing for you. Only so much in a word, this manna of rarities from heaven is your daily bread. I must move onwards.

Thirdly, a work is then carried on mysteriously, when it is carried on *contra naturam*. What English shall I have to reach this expression with all? When a work is carried on contrarily and contradictorily; it is a hard phrase, but so overflowing are the mysteries of mercy, which God is now working among us, that certainly our English tongue is grown too narrow to lend us words to express them. I must therefore use the word *contradictorily*. Contradictory, what is that? That is, when a work is promoted and carried on by its contraries. I must show it by an instance. When the manner of a work runs like Samson's riddle, Judges 14:14, "out of the eater came forth meat, and out of the strong sweetness." That the eater should yield meat, and the strong give out sweetness, this is such a riddle that a strict logician hearing it would be ready to cry out *implicat*, it is a contradiction *in adjecto*; yet so it is when enemies become those who further a work against themselves, and that is common you see among us.

Samson's riddle does not express it sufficiently, so I will add another expression out of the Psalmist; it is in

Psalm 112:4, "Unto the upright there aroused light in darkness." It is according to nature that the dawning springs out of the night, and that the more perfect day arises out of that dawning is still according to nature, because the increase is gradual. But when light shall arise immediately out of darkness, when high noon shall suddenly leap out of midnight, such a jump is against nature, and you must call it a mystery; because it is held as a *maxim* among naturalists, that *natura nihil agit per saltum*, the motion of nature is not by leaps, but by paces. So Mark 4:28, "first the blade, then the ear, after that the full corn in the ear." Therefore as often as we shall see a branch (I mean a fruit of providence) like the rod of Aaron, that in one night was budded and brought forth buds and bloomed blossoms, and yielded almonds (Numbers 17:8) so often let us confess with the Psalmist, "this is the Lord's doing, and it is marvelous in our eyes."

Yes, but when, or where did we ever see such things as these?

I would give some few particular instances under this head of salvation through contrarieties and contradictions.

1. As when enemies do further a work against themselves, yes and that by fighting against it. This contradiction we have found true ever since the beginning of our present troubles. The enemy by projecting and fighting *against reformation*, has both hastened and heightened it more than ourselves could (perhaps would) have done in that time. When there had been a talk a while often the beginning of this parliament, of some solemn way of uniting the kingdom's by some special association in those crazy times, the enemy by increasing our dangers and obstructing (as I remember) the proceedings quicken as into a protestation. And because that obligation was easily broken (ah lamentable!) by the generality of men who deserted their own protection and remedy, there some enemy would never leave adding one horrid provocation to another, by fighting against the parliament, denying them a being, proclaiming them rebels, and owning the diabolical

rebels of Ireland as good subjects, to cut their throats; until by such sharp provocations as these, they had spurred and switched the three kingdoms into a most *solemn oath and covenant* for a *complete reformation.* The men would not suffer us (if we would) only to pair and clip prelacy, no; they will have it plucked up *root and branch.* They will not suffer the three kingdoms to rest in several kinds and pitches of government and worship, but they will have *one true reformed uniformity* in these and all other churches of Christ. So their rage has abundantly ripened the work. This is seemingly contradictory.

2. When one and the same thing is at once helpful to God's people, and hurtful to the enemy. As it is said of the angel, and the pillar of the cloud, Exodus 14:19, "and the angel of God which went before the camp of Israel, removed and went behind them, and the pillar of the cloud went from before their faces and stood behind them." Verse 20, and it came between the camp of the Egyptians, and the camp of Israel, and it was a cloud of darkness to them, but it gave light by night to these, so that the one came not near the other all the night. Such helpful hindering occurents have we often met with, that have proved like the extraordinary frost that (it is said)

suddenly happened in the north at the coming in of the present Scottish army; it blocked up the ways of the enemy by abundance of snow, that they could not plunder and fire as they intended; but it gave an unexpected passage of ice over the river to our brethren and their carriages. Many of the same acts might be shown, which on the one hand showed the Lord's presence with his people, (as I have seen some two faced pictures) and on the other hand in the same side the picture of Satan for the ruin of the enemies.

3. When losses are gains. I have touched on this before; let me only add the instances of the two great public battles that have been fought in this cause, at Keinton and at Newbery. In the beginning of both battles, it is said, we were somewhat worse, to show that England had offended the Lord, and therefore our father beat us. But then we conquered the enemy too, to imply that the Lord would own his own cause and people not withstanding their failings. So *victim vicimus*, by being first worst, we were made more than conquerors (*periissemus nifi periissemus*) being beaten we got the day. This examination is preparatory to the following lessons.

A Second Use

Use 2. To inform and satisfy. Let no man think that it is strange that there is so much shrinking, stretching and warping from the right party in the present times and controversies. No marvel if mere sensitive common worldliness and carnal politics do fall off from this divine and supernatural cause and task. Such poor pur-blind creatures were mistaken in this work at their first coming on. It was their lot to be cast on the parliament side, and in that lot, they looked on carnal and selfish ends and arguments; on the loaves and the bag that were to be gotten by Christ's service, I mean majority of number, probability of short dispatch and long preferment's after, drew them to the right party. But finding the business to be a holy mystery, finding that the Lord carried his work thorough hills and dales of land and seas; yes and that they should be forced to deny themselves, to adventure all, to cross the stream. Here they went away sorrowing, this was too hard a saying, and they could not bear it. To speak plainly. Honorable and beloved, in the beginning of this parliament when the Lord gave you a plentiful breakfast of most smooth and happy successes in your first proceedings, by this to strengthen you for the hard day's work and long journey that was to come in setting down our *Westminster Standards and Confession*, (as he gave a double breakfast to Elijah when he was to travel without meat forty days and forty nights, to Horeb the Mount of God, 1 Kings 19:5, 7-8). You may remember that in those prosperous days you were compassed about with swarming proselytes, and seeming patriots of all bores and sizes. But how did many of those pretenders fail you in the heat as brooks in summer?

Some of them were mere sensitive friends. This like an incredulous thorn would believe and adventure no farther than their senses of sight and feeling and lead them. They would have the ground of their faith at their fingers end, as Job 20:25, and they were drawn on merely as that mixed multitude (or a great mixture) that went out of Egypt with the children of Israel, because of the miracles and mercies that there were wrought, Exodus 12:38. Therefore, later, after when your hardships began, this same mixture was at first fallen to lusting, as that Egyptian mixture did. Numbers 11:4 and the mixed multitude that was among them fell to lusting. So your mere sensitive friends fell off.

Others were led by human reason and political convictions. These stuck to parliaments, laws and privileges, as Orpah to her mother in law Naomi, that is, while she continued Naomi (*pleasant*) but when by afflictions she became Marah (*bitter*) then they (as Orpah, Ruth 1:14-20) wept and kissed their mother in law, but *departed*.

Shortly, a last sort were of false or faint hearted professors, led with some light of religion; they either broke off like Demas, or warped off like Paul's acquaintance at his first appearing before Nero, 1 Timothy 4:16.

But would you know the cause of all this failing? Surely it was nothing but this (as before) those shallow headed narrow hearted carnality were puzzled in this hard lesson of a *mystery*. The mere natural man can read in the book of the creatures, it is so fair a print in capital letters. The prudential man can perceive the character, and construe the language of common providence. And so far they went with you. But they were not so much, as children learning their a-b-c's in the Lord's *archivis* (as they say) in his manuscripts, in his brachigraphy. I mean in the strange language and abstruse character of reformation, and mysterious Babylonish redemptions; they wanted both dictionaries and spectacle in those particulars. Then do not let the apostasy of carnality cast any disparagement on this glorious mystery. That's a second use.

Thirdly, if God's great salvation of his people, especially that from Babylon be carried on in a mystery, then away with that great old English sin of *carnality*, away with carnality in both extremes, on the right hand, and on the left hand, away with carnal confidence, and carnal dissidence.

First, away with carnal confidence; do not be too much lifted up with outward supplies, with outward strength and successes; but remember that the frame of this work is mysterious and spiritual. Therefore, for us to build our hopes on things that are merely carnal must necessarily be a sin, both heterogeneous and most improper. We have been taught by experience, that fleshly and worldly advantages here have contributed little to the principal part of this work. Commonly (here and there) the race has not been to the swift, nor the battle to the strong, nor yet bread to men of understanding, Ecclesiastes 9:11. We never had (I think) too few armies for any service and engagement since we began; perhaps sometimes through the corruption of our hearts we have had too many, as God said to Gideon, "the people that are with thee are too many for me to give the Medianites into their hands." Consider further, that carnal confidence begets carnal dissidence, as the hot and cold fits in an aguish fever mutually intend and heighten one another. Therefore away with carnality on the right hand, and with carnal confidence.

And then on the other hand, by the same reason, away also with carnal dissidence in case of the lack of outward supplies and successes. Remember the doctrine that has said that this work is a work of faith, and not of sense; and continual experience evidences that when we are weak we are strong. My meaning is, that we should not be any longer like weather glasses suffering our hopes and spirits to rise and fall according to the tidings of good and bad successes – things we see or success we see with just our eyes; that we should not live on carnal faith, or on the air of news and intelligence. But let our hopes be like the life of the saints that is hidden with Christ in God. Let them have a surer foundation than anything that base carnality can suggest. Do not let our confidence, like heavy Eli, fall backward and break their neck on the report of every defeat. Had Eli born up through that blast, he might have seen that the loss of the ark, was in conclusion, the advantage of Israel. The Philistines were never so shamefully beaten as by that victory; for that very ark when it was set up in the house of Dagon conquered the idol in his own temple, for his head and both the palms of his hands were cut off on the threshold, and only the stump of Dagon was left whole. Yes and the Philistines themselves were beat at last, as it were to bribe their prisoner with golden mice and tumors, to be gone; and were forced to send the ark home again, with shame, and cost enough.

But there are many specious arguments given, in excuse of such carnal dissidence.

As first one might ask, O! But there is great opposition, many, mighty stubborn enemies there are against us?

This is good evidence that you are about a choice piece of church work. Show me a reformation (I think there is scarcely one) in the book of God, or in our protestant histories, that went on *without difficulties and obstructions*. So that these very crags and bogs which you pass thorough in the way, are not discouragements, but *way marks*, that is, *certain signs* that you are right in the old reformation way that has ever been trodden. So Asa had no sooner set on a reformation in Judah, (2 Chronicles 14 and 2 Chronicles 15) by covenanting strictly with God; by pulling down idolatry, and by removing queen Maacha her capuchins, but two thousand Ethiopians are let in on his kingdom, as though hell itself had been let loose. So king Hezekiah, after these things (says the text) and the establishment of them, (2 Chronicles 32:1) that is, after three chapters full of reformation that you read of before. Then Senacherib, king of Assyria, came and entered into Judah with a great army. Therefore these bogs, crags, and brambles, are approved way marks and encouragements.

Again, you must give parting devil's leave to tear and scream when they are to be immediately cast out. The evil spirit will have one pull with the possessed person, when he is packing. You know it is so said, Revelation 12:12, *the devil is come down having great wrath, because he knows that he has but a short time.* And so in Mark 9:26, when the dumb devil was to be cast out (as how many dumb devils are now casting out of many parishes in the land!) he tore the man, and made him look as though he was as one dead. This we must look for, it is a sign that the devil is leaving.

But the work is tedious; O! is it this prolixity which wears us out?

This is but proportional, when a sickness has been so long a growing and crusting in the kingdom, it would be dangerous to purge it suddenly; our body politic would hardly bear the strength of the medicine. This prolixity therefore is a wise mercy.

Add that all this prolixity is usual in such *solid* church work. The return of the Jews from Babylon, taking in the whole of it, that is, the two pieces, spiritual and temporal (the building of the temple, and of the wall of the city) was on the wheel, as I remember, thorough some seven princes reigns, *viz.* Cyrus, Cambyses, Darius Histaspis, Xerxes or Ahasuerus, Artaxerxes Longimanus, Darius Nothus and Artaxerxes Mnemon. But our reformation as yet is but in the reign of the sixth since it began. The number may be thus computed; *viz.* Henry 8,

Edward 6, Queen Mary, Queen Elizabeth, King James, and our sovereign that now reigned. Therefore this prolixity has a pattern, it is usual.

Lastly, it is also profitable and advantageous for us. It is true, when a river runs with many turnings and windings, the vessel that fails on her makes the longer voyage from place to place; but those turnings and meanders are abundantly profitable to the bordering inhabitants, both to prevent inundations, by breaking the strength of the floods, and to multiply rich meadows and pastures by its various indentures. So there is the less danger, and the more fruitfulness by the prolixity of this mysterious work.

But in the meanwhile we are undone in our estates? That was Micha's language when he had lost his idol. Take heed that we do not idolize our estates and make them our gods, and then indeed we shall cry out and say as he did, what have we more?

But further, they are but exchanges of temporal for spirituals, earth for gold. Has not your soul gained something by these troubles in recompense of that which they purse has lost? What, not some experience, some humiliation, faith or holiness?

However, your God is left with you still, and that God is able to fetch sweet out of bitter, good out of evil, not only out of the evil of punishment, but out of the evil of sin itself. In short, this doctrine answers all carnal objections that can be moved. But I must hasten on.

Are God's great salvations carried on in a mystery? Then in the fourth place, let us be advised to look on this work as it is to be carried on, that is, spiritually, extraordinary, mysteriously; that so we may not be mistaken in our way and task, as many carnal politicians and formal neuters have mistaken the work, and so miscarried and fallen away at last.

Consider, honorable and beloved, it is not a journey, but a voyage, which the Lord has put you on. You know the difference; in a voyage there is one and the same common safety or ship wreck to all the passengers, they must swim or sink together. Not so in a land journey. In a voyage there is much hard ship by lodging, diet, straightness and dangers by rocks, sands, pirates and tempests. So you see it is not so in a land journey. But especially I call your task a voyage, in respect of the various motions and path less ways into which your work carries you. Sometimes the seaman is forced to board it to and fro, so that an unskillful spectator would think that he goes forth and back. Another while he is sane to strike all his sails and to drive a hull, so that he seems utterly to neglect his vessel; yet all this while he is at his work, and makes way as he can. But above all the rest, you must remember that in a voyage there are no lanes, no foot paths, no highway Mercury's to direct the seamen; all their directions must be fetched from the pole and stars compared with their card, their compass, and the touched needle; their path lies in heaven, not below. So you have a God above, a guide in heaven, you have his word and will for your card and compass; and your own hearts touched within you, still standing God-ward. These must, these can guide your through a sea of miseries and mysteries to the haven of reformation and deliverance where you would be. Let these guides and guidance be closely followed, and then no matter for waves and winds, no matter for sea sickness, it is a good sign of the progress of the ship, and it is good medicine to the passenger.

What do We Learn from This?

But suppose all the premises are granted, namely that this work in its carriage is so spiritual, casual, and contradictory, so truly mysterious; how then may we so order and lesson ourselves, as to discharge our duties in such difficult service? This mystery does seem to leave us in a mere muse of contemplation; what action or practice is there left to us to be performed in this case? What *doing* lessons may be fetched from here?

There are some sure practical lessons to be learned from the mysterious carriage of our present salvations; and that I may show them the more fully, you must know that in this work there are two parts.

Aliquid divinum. Something divine, and supernatural, which is chiefly the Lord's end.

Aliquid humanum. Something more human and secular, which is man's ends and aims.

The Great Lesson to be Learned

Now the great lesson in general which we are to learn, is to stick and cleave to all God's ends above any of our own. It was a great error of the Jews, and Haggai complied of it, Haggai 1:2, that they fell a building of their own houses, but let the house of God lie waste; therefore the Lord is sane to curse, and cross them in their own selfish designs, even in the fruit of the field, and in their very meat, drink, and cloth, as you may read verse 6. You have sown much, and bring in little, you eat, and have not enough; you drink, but you are not filled with drink; you cloth yes, but there is none warm, and he that earns wages puts it into a broken bag. God crossed them in things nearest to them, that so they might look more after his part of the work. And indeed it is the wonderful mercy of God to us, that these two parts of the work (reformation and deliverance) are so twisted tougher, that we are not able to separate them. God has now so indissolubly interwoven the reforming of religion with the settlement of laws and liberties that we cannot pick off the latter, and leave the former. Otherwise (I fear) we should hear this, have been playing the children, that use to eat of their honey, and then throw the bread to the dogs. But our Father has so wisely ordered the whole, that if we will have no reformation of religion; we shall have no more laws, parliaments, liberties, nor privileges.

Therefore it will be our wisdom, to look chiefly after the Lord's part of the work.

But, what is God's part, end, and aim?

I answer, the Lord's ends, designs, or desires, (as I may call them) in this great work, may be considered two ways, either generally, or particularly.

1. Works of piety. The Lord absolutely requires the reformation of religion at this time, both in doctrine, worship, discipline, and government, in the church. We must out with idols, not only those in wood, stone, or glass, that is in walls and windows; but those living idols that are in pews and in some pulpits, they must out; I mean all idol shepherds, and dumb dogs. While Israel was without a teaching priest, they were without law. A preacher less people will be a lawless people. In short, the Lord would have you to demolish all high places, and not to leave so much as the stump of Dagon remaining. Yes to bury all the relics of Romish Jezabel, even the skull, and the feet, and the palms of her hands. Also the Lord does expect that you should promote the last solemn league and covenant, that triple cable of the three kingdoms, by which the anchor of our hope is fastened, that threefold cord that binds all these kingdoms together and to God;

and is like that golden chain with which the tyrants (when Alexander beleaguered them) bound fast their tutelary god, Apollo; for fear he would leave their city. So if you do first build the Lord's house and do become faithful midwives to his laboring church, then doubtless will the Lord deal well with you, and will make you houses, as Exodus 1:17, 20-21.

1. Works of justice are a part of God's general design at this time, you cannot but remember the service of Phinehas in executing of judgment when it was a sad time with Israel, and the double reward that followed; public to the state, (the plague was stayed), and private to his own family, the service of God in the church was particularly entailed on him and his posterity, Number 25, and blessed be God, that you have now put into the scales of justice, the archest prelate of the land. Believe it, such services as these, are the way to procure to us a valley of Achor for a door of hope, even then when we do fly before the enemy, as Joshua 7:26, when Achan was found out and put to his trial according to justice, the wrath of God was stopped; and the late victorious city of Ai is soon taken in.

2. The Lord now calls for works and acts of mercy too, that is, that you take special notice of the most doing and suffering places and persons, that have laid out themselves in this cause to the utmost, that like that poor widow, 1 Kings 17, have made a cake for the prophet, out of their handful of meal, and on this are much distressed and scanted. You remember what David said to Abiathar, when all the persons of his father's house were slain by Saul, "abide thou with me, fear not, for he that seeks my life, seeks thy life, but with me shall thou be in safety." Much more ought those faithful persons, towns, cities, and countries to be relieved that have been most active and passive for God and the kingdom in this cause.

And here, oh how gladly could I weep in a parenthesis, for, and over the country of my nativity, the place of my father's sepulchers which lies waste, where so many houses and places are consumed with fire! Oh the unparallel misery of the still declining west! Is it nothing to you, all ye that pass by! *Behold and see if there is any sorrow likened to our sorrow, which is done to us, where the Lord has afflicted us, in the day of his fierce anger,* Lamentations 1:12. Could I but draw forth in their due colors the doings and sufferings of those parts of the land, I am persuaded (whatever fame may chatter) that I should prevail with the driest heart in this great assembly, to contribute, at least a tear towards our relief and true succor, I confess the Lord is righteous, for we have rebelled against his mouth; but yet for doing and suffering in this great cause, I am persuaded those parts may be ranked among the foremost of the kingdom. And my humble desire is, that accordingly they may have place in your prayers and cares. So let the Lord's general and public designs and ends be first considered and promoted.

But secondly, I must tell you that God has other collateral designs, (and as I may call them), intermediate ends in this strange work, which we ought also to observe and further to our uttermost; that's the second practical lesson. As it is with those that labor to find out the philosophers stone by distillations, their ultimate and principal end is to make gold, yet by the way and collaterally they find out many rare experiments and excellent chemical extractions, which are of precious use and value.

So is it in this great work of God, his grand principal design is public salvation, both by reformation and deliverance; but he has many collateral, occasional, intermediate designs and effects which he intended and produced by the way. As for instance he had (suppose) a design, and an experiment to be made on his own church and people, as to try the particular graces of this or that saint, what strength of faith, what depth of humility, what latitude of patience there is in their hearts. Or if not for trial, then I suppose for purging, or correcting, or improving; and it should be our care to record such experiments for after times, whether they tend to our humiliation, or to our consolation. Another while the Lord had a design on the enemy (as I showed in my grounds) to make him fill up the measure of sin, and confusion of face or person. The open adversaries must have their full load, and the secret neuters must be detected, as it is said, Luke 2:35. "Yea a sword shall pierce through your own side, that the thoughts of many hearts may be revealed." The stabs and gashes of the present sword opened and let out many secret thoughts. Who so is wise, and will observe these things, even they shall understand the loving kindness of the Lord, Psalm 107.43.

Let the closing branch of application be a cordial. There is a cordial in this doctrine, and I hope a cordial is not unseasonable at a fast, so as it enables us the more heartily to go through the work of the day. Then here is a melting cordial, for by the mysterious carriage of our present work we may easily gather that God is now on some great salvation, yes on a salvation from Western Babylon. The whole work in all its progress looks exactly like the foretold destruction of Babylon. For our God, even while he hides himself, is still the Savior of this Israel. My encouragement therefore shall lie in the same words (for so God has directed us) that you had in the morning from my reverend brother; it seems God will have us both to drive the same nail that it may be sent home to the head. It is in Haggai 2:4, "Yet now be strong, O Zerubbabbel, says the Lord, and be strong O Joshua, son of Josedech the high priest, and be strong O ye people of the land and work for I am with you, says the Lord of Hosts." Here is something for all ranks, parliament men, Zerubbabel, assembly of divines, Joshua. And all the people, the whole commonalty. The strength of the argument lies in that sweet parenthesis at last, and I shall close with the handling of it "for I am with you, says the Lord of Hosts." In which you may observe but these two blasts to fill your sails.

First, who is the master builder, the architect that employs you, and accordingly you know whether to go for your wages? "I am with you, says the Lord of Hosts." Would any man ask a more honorable serve than under the Lord of Hosts? For *honor est in honorante*, and it comes properly by arms. Certainly, the Lord never put a more honorable employment into the hands of the sons of England, than he has put this day into your hands to set down these *Standards*. What, to be champions for God, to be builders, factors, reformers for the whole protestant cause and world! How many of our zealous ancestors have cast in their prayers, tears and blood, to entail on us but the preparations and probabilities of this great work? How did they long to have seen one of these days a fair off, but did not see them? David was not permitted to build the temple, but God reserved that work for his son Jedidiah (for so the Lord himself called Solomon) who was the beloved of the Lord. Do you think it a small thing to be God's *Jedidiah* in this respect? To be builders of a house to the God of heaven is your honor. But that is but half.

Secondly, look on God's ownership of the work. This Lord of Hosts will be with you. Would any man in the world desire a clearer promise than was this to Zerubbabel, *I will be with you, upon my word, upon my honor, upon my deity I will be with you?*

No (you will say) we would not wish a surer word to ourselves, but that was made peculiarly to the Jews. Had we but such a promise, we would stick at nothing. Had we but the faith of heaven so engaged to us?

I answer, you have it as they had it, no, in some sort I may say, and you have it *more fully.* For they had it promised, and therefore it was in future, yet to come. But you have it, *in presenti,* in hand. Open your eyes and behold your encouragements; the Lord speaks to you in deeds, and faith, *Lo, I Am with you in all this work, you may feel my presence on every occasion.*

Let me reason with you a little before the Lord concerning his providence over you. Did ever the Lord so clearly, so visibly own and English parliament as he has owned you? Do but first look back on your first convention. Are you not the very birth of the prayers of many generations? Were you not as a brand snatched out of the fire kindled between England and Scotland? Just as were those reformers in the Babylonish captivity. Is not this a brand (God says, Zecharriah 3:2) plucked out of the fire? Suppose a man of judgment coming into a room where there is a fire burning, and he runs hastily to the fire side, snatched thence a piece of wood, and endeavors by all means to extinguish the flame that is on it; will not every rational man presently conclude that he intended that piece for some special service? In this sense (as I conceive) is that metaphor used in that place; *is not this a brand plucked out of the fire?* As if the Lord should have said, *have I plucked Joshua out of the fire of Babylon and so this parliament out of the fire of the two kingdoms, when they were in combustion some three years since, to cast them into the consuming flames again at last?* No surely, that is not the Lord's usual manner.

And as for your convention, so secondly consider the progress of providence in your settlement. How has God fastened you as a nail in a sure place? This is an argument in which the Jews comforted themselves at the time of their return from Babylon, Ezra 9:8, and now for a little space, grace has been showed from the Lord our God, to leave us a remnant to escape, and to give us a nail in his holy place. Surely, you are our remnant escaped, without which we had been as Sodom, and as the inhabitants of Gomorrah; and you are fastened as a nail in a sure place, by a special act for your continuance, above all former parliaments. Well did the Lord foresee both what a great work himself would put into your hands; and what great oppositions you should meet with all? When God fastens a nail of power and authority in a sure place, he does usually intend to hand some extraordinary weight and glory on it, as it is said of Eliakim, who was a figure of Christ, Isa. 22:23, "and I will fasten him as a nail in a sure place," verse 24. And they shall hang on him all the glory of his father's house, the off spring and the issue, all vessels (of small quantity) from the vessels of cups, even to all the vessels of flagons.

Thirdly, besides your extraordinary convention and unparallel fastening. Consider lastly what the Lord has done (for you and by you) since you came together.

1. For you, how often has he given a new life to your whole house, collectively and in common, and that sometimes by rescuing you from bloody assassinates? Oh! Let the 4th of January, 1641 be to you as the 5th of November 1605. Sometimes by giving you the victory in the open field, when your lives lay at stake in the battle, a

in both those general battles at Keinton and Newbery. Besides, how many of your members distributive have had their lives given to them as a particular prey, being snatched out of natural and violent deaths since they began this service? I do not speak this that your hearts should be lifted up within you, but that they may be lifted up in the ways of the Lord.

2. Next consider what God has done by your also; did ever the Lord do so much work of this kind in so short a time (however we think the tie to be long) since protestant reformation began in the Christian world? If so, then I was mistaken or forgetful in reading that exact record of reformation since Luther's beginning.

So much work done (you will say?) *alas, alas, what is there done all this while, besides the kindling of an unnatural war?* As for reformation there is nothing completely perfected in that to this day, for want of the royal ascent?

I answer first, yet there is somewhat already done, the best, the spiritual part of the work does still go on, and the reason why we see it not, is because we look to the politic and outward part of the business, more than to the inward and spiritual part. For this abundantly goes on still even in the middle of all the storms. The wall is building through in troublous times, as Daniel 9:25. Have you even been on the shore at low water, and there observed the coming in of the tide; you shall see first one little wave creeping forwards, and presently retiring itself again, and so another and another, but everyone does still retreat as soon, as fast, as it did advance, so that a diligent observer viewing the water in motion, may easily believe that the flood does not at all increase. But set a mark, or keep your standing near the wash of the waves, for a short time, and then you shall quickly and clearly see and feel that all this while it is flowing water, and a non-insensibly it will be a full sea. So in the present great work, though there appears to be a vicissitude of victories between God and his enemies, though success seems to a carnal eye promiscuously to go and come, yet stand still a while and look on the spiritual, the religious part of the work, and you shall find the waters of the sanctuary still flowing and increasing, as in Ezekiel's vision, chapter 47. First they were to the ankles, next to the knees, then to the loins, and lastly they were a river that could not be passed over. I mean that the work of reformation still goes on; there we do get ground, as to perfect a protestation into a covenant, to ripen an impeachment into a root and branch, and in a word, to settle an assembly of divines as a general refiner's fire to try all metals in the church.

But secondly, whereas you say, that nothing is yet completely perfected for lack of the royal assent.

Know this that the Lord carries on this frame of building in like manner as Solomon's temple was built. Do you not remember how Solomon built his temple? You may see it in 1 Kings 6:7. And the house when it in was building was built of stone, made ready before it was brought there, so that there was neither hammer or ax, or any tool of iron heard in the house while it was in building. And in Kings 5:6 it is said that the cedar trees were hewers and made fit in Lebanon, and then they were brought down by water to the place where they were to be used. And verse 15 you shall read that Solomon had three score and ten thousand that bare burdens, and four score thousand that were hewers in the mountains. Just so is the building of this Christian Protestant temple carried on? The Lord prepares one piece of the building in Germany, there he has had thousands of hewers of wood and sellers of trees these twenty years, to cut down some and to square out others for this structure; he has others, that bear burdens in Ireland, and they shall bring in another kind of materials. And then Scotland does come in perhaps with solder and cement, they shall further us in covenanting; and at last, when all these materials shall be brought in place by water (by our prayers) then you shall see a glorious temple set up, perhaps in one week, no, in a day or a night, and that without the noise of ax or hammer, or any tool or iron. You are showing in the house of parliament; the divines are squaring in their assembly, in one night the Lord is able to work on the heart of the King (for he has it in his hand) and to deliver him into the bosom of you his faithful counsel, then the whole work may suddenly be passed and finished.

Onward therefore noble builders, onward, up and be doing your several parts; your God is invincible; your cause in invincible, and nothing is so like to hazard us as not adventuring. Your labor, your cost, your adventures, cannot be in vain, in the Lord. Oh remember, Peter is used there in a spiritual way; I shall borrow it in this sense, 1 Peter 1:13, "hope unto the end," that is, adventure for God and trust him to the uttermost, to the brink, to the edge, to the end of all means and possibilities, to the last inch of the candle, to the last dust of meals in the barrel, to the least drop of oil in the bottom of the cruise. So did that poor widow. So did Abraham, Genesis 22. First his son Isaac, and himself went, verse 8 *to the mount*, he built an altar, laid the wood in order, *bound* Isaac his son, laid him on the altar on the wood (yet the trial is not come to the edge, the brink, the uttermost). But lastly, verse 10, "Abraham stretched forth his hand and took the knife to slay his son." This indeed was hope against hope, as, Romans 4:18. This was trusting to the end. But was Abraham a loser by it? I am sure that King Saul lost a kingdom for lack of an hour faith, and adventuring further, as 1 Samuel 13:10. Labor therefore to trust the Lord to the uttermost end of means, yes above, and against them, rather than sin against him by unbelief. Labor (In three words) to play the Solomon's, the David's, the Samson's in this work.

Two Lessons to be Learned

First to play like Solomon. That is, as you have begun their reformation, so do your utmost endeavor to finish it in your days. Believe it, when you have built the

House of God, you shall have both leave and ability to build your own houses. You read so of Solomon in 1 Kings 7:1. When he had built the House of God, then he built his own house, and a house for his wife, and the house of the forest of Lebanon.

Or if you may not be the Solomon, yet labor to be *David* in this work, you know God denied to David the honor of building his temple. Yet David would not utterly be put off; he will be doing as much as he may. First he offered himself to the work, 1 Chronicles 28:15ff, and has offered gold, silver, brass and iron.

Next, he draws in his nobles and all his people, as deeply as he can. And thirdly, he leaves also a stock of prayers behind him, 2 Chronicles 29:10. Yes, finally he gives a charge to his son Solomon to go through with the work, 2 Chronicles 28:11. And leaves him a pattern of the house. And even those very preparations and purposes of David were richly rewarded, 2 Samuel 7:4. So if the Lord for our sins and unbelief has decreed that your carcass's and ours shall fall in the wilderness, and that we shall only see this Canaan a far off; yet let these two lessons be learned.

1. Let every soul be careful to avoid all those sins that are won't to draw down this punishment of not entering; see some of them, 1 Corinthians 10:6-7. Beware of lusting, of idolatry, of tempting of God, of murmuring.

2. Let us labor to contribute and store up materials for those that shall finish the work after us.

And lastly, if you may not be permitted to do so much as Solomon, or as David, yet at last, at least let us endeavor to play like Samson in this work. What is that? You shall read it, Judges 16:29. When Samson could not conquer the Philistines, could not make a thorough salvation of it, as he desired, yet the text says, "he called unto the Lord, and said, remember me I pray thee, and strengthen me I pray thee only this once, that I may be at once avenged of the Philistines for my two eyes. And Samson took hold of the two middle pillars, on which the house stood, and on which it was born up, and he said, let me die with the Philistines and he bowed himself with all his might, and the house fell on all the people that were therein; so the dead which he show at his death, were more than those which he show in his life." My meaning is this; better for us if we cannot out live antichrist, outlive Babylon, and the enemies of reformation; to adventure (as far as we are) ourselves to death in the cause. Let us take hold of the pillars of the house of Dagon, of the temple of antichrist, and say, *now let me die with antichrist, Rome and Babylon.* Better so (I say) than to live with the eyes of our religion put out, and to grind in the mill of slavery. For by this means the children that shall come after us shall sit on our tombs and say that they had active parents, which with their blood and carcasses did dress the ground for reformation to spring up after them. For my own part, I shall say, he that is of so base of spirit that can be content to outlive Protestantism and parliaments, let it be his punishment to outlive them. I do not desire to fall under the just reproof of a heathen:

> *Vita est avidus quisquis noivult,*
>
> *Mando secum pereunte mori.*

Conclusion

To finish this all. Be strong in the Lord and in the power of his might; on the eternal and infinite faith of the Trinity, and in the word of Jehovah, your loss for his sake shall be repaid. Will you take that word? Then there are two special promises which I will commend to you in the close of all. Oh that they were written over the doors of the houses of parliament!

Matthew 19:29, "Everyone that has forsaken houses, or brethren, or sister, or father, or mother, or wife, or children, or lands (*can you reckon up anything else?*) for my name's sake, he shall receive a hundred fold (*God will pay him the very interest*) and he shall inherit everlasting life (*to boot*)."

Matthew 8:35, "Whosoever will save his life shall lose it, but he that loses his life for my sake shall find it."

If these places deceive an active believer at last, then let it be written on my grave, "Here lies that minister that was mistaken in his God and gospel."

FINIS

www.ingramcontent.com/pod-product-compliance
Lightning Source LLC
Chambersburg PA
CBHW022159080426
42734CB00006B/509